M000022352

TEATIME RECIPES

Traditional Welsh Cakes
Cacennau Traddodiadol
o Gymru

with illustrations by
A. R. Quinton

SALMON

Index

Cover pictures: *front:* The Bridge, Beddgelert *back:* Tintern Abbey
title page: The SwallowFalls, Betws-y-Coed

Copyright, Printed and Published by J. Salmon Ltd., Sevenoaks, England ©

Llanddarog Fair Cakes
Teisennau Ffair Llanddarog

Traditionally sold as fairings, these little cakes from Carmarthenshire contain beer and are topped with dried fruit.

6 oz. self raising flour	**2 oz. caster sugar**
Pinch of salt	**3 dessertspoons of beer**
4 oz. butter	**1 oz. sultanas**
1 oz. currants	

Set oven to 375°F or Mark 5. Sift the flour and salt together into a bowl, then rub in the butter until the mixture resembles breadcrumbs. Stir in the sugar, then add the beer and mix to a soft dough. Roll out on a lightly floured surface to about ½ inch thick and cut into rounds with a plain cutter. Mix the sultanas and currants together and press on to the tops of the rounds. Bake for 15 minutes and cool on a wire rack. Serve plain.

Bara Brith
Fruit Loaf

*This popular Welsh fruit cake is called Bara or bread from its similarity
of appearance to a bread loaf.*

10 oz. mixed dried fruit	**Grated rind of 1 lemon**
⅔ pint hot tea (no milk)	**12 oz. self raising wholemeal flour**
3 oz. soft brown sugar	**1 teaspoon mixed spice**

1 large egg

Soak the mixed dried fruit in the hot tea, cover and leave to stand overnight. Next day, set oven to 350°F or Mark 4 and grease and line a 2 lb. loaf tin. Strain the fruit and reserve the liquid. Mix together the fruit with the other ingredients in a bowl, adding the reserved liquid a little at a time until a soft, dropping consistency is achieved. Pour the mixture into the tin and bake for 45-55 minutes until risen and firm to the touch. Cool and serve sliced and buttered.

Anglesey Bakestones
Teisennau Criwsion Môn

Made with lard, these little cakes were traditionally cooked on a bakestone or griddle.

8 oz. flour
½ teaspoon baking powder
Pinch of salt

4 oz. lard
1 egg, beaten
Milk

Sift together into a bowl the flour, baking powder and salt, then rub in the lard until the mixture resembles breadcrumbs. Add the egg and sufficient milk to form a soft dough. Heat a greased griddle or heavy based frying pan and place tablespoons of the mixture on the griddle, flattening them slightly. Cook for about 5 minutes on each side, until golden brown. Serve hot, plain or with butter.

Brecon Light Cakes
Cacen Olau Aberhonddu

These little pancakes or drop scones are delicately flavoured with orange juice.

4 oz. self raising flour	2 tablespoons orange juice
½ teaspoon salt	2-3 tablespoons milk
2 oz. caster sugar	1 oz. butter or margarine for frying
2 eggs	1 oz. soft brown sugar

Beat the eggs together with half the orange juice. Sift the flour and the salt into a mixing bowl and add the caster sugar. Add the egg mixture, stirring well. Beat in the milk to produce a fairly thin batter. Melt the butter or margarine in a heavy frying pan. When it begins to sizzle, drop in tablespoons of the mixture, allowing room to spread (2-3 inches). Cook on each side until golden brown. Drain on kitchen paper. Serve sprinkled with brown sugar and orange juice.

Welsh Cakes
Pice ar y maen

Popular throughout Wales, these little cakes, originally cooked on a heated bakestone, were often served to travellers on their arrival at an inn. In North Wales they are known as Teisen Gri.

1 lb. flour	4 oz. lard
1 teaspoon baking powder	7 oz. sugar
1 pinch allspice	4 oz. seedless raisins
1 pinch salt	2 eggs, beaten
4 oz. butter	Milk to mix

Caster sugar to sprinkle

Stir together the flour, baking powder, allspice and salt in a large bowl. Rub in the butter and the lard. Add the sugar and raisins. Beat the eggs and add to the mixture, with a little milk, to make a fairly stiff dough. Roll out on a lightly floured surface to a thickness of about ¼ inch and cut into 2 inch rounds with a pastry cutter. Cook on a greased griddle or heavy based frying pan for about 3 minutes each side until golden brown. Sprinkle with sugar and serve warm.

Sage and Leek Bread
Bara Saets a Chennin

A wholemeal loaf with sage and leek for an unusual flavour and texture.

8 oz. strong white flour	1 teaspoon dried sage
8 oz. strong wholemeal flour	1 large leek, washed and finely chopped
1 sachet dried yeast	1 oz. butter
1 teaspoon salt	½ pint tepid milk
Pepper	1 teaspoon sesame seeds

Set oven to 400°F or Mark 6. Melt the butter in a saucepan and gently soften the chopped leek. Put the flours, salt, dried yeast, pepper and sage into a large bowl. Make a well and pour in the leek and butter and tepid milk. Beat well together until the dough leaves the sides of the bowl cleanly. Turn out on to a lightly floured surface and knead well for 10 minutes until smooth. Place in a clean bowl, cover and leave in a warm place for about one hour until it doubles in bulk. Turn out and knead well again. Divide into two. Shape into rounds and place on a greased baking sheet. Brush with a little milk and sprinkle with sesame seeds. Cover and leave in a warm place to rise until double in bulk (30-40 minutes). Bake for 30 minutes. When cooked the loaves should be golden brown and sound hollow when tapped on the bottom. Cool on a wire rack.

Caerphilly Scones
Sgonau Caerffili

These scones make use of Caerphilly's famous cheese flavoured with chopped chives.

8 oz. self raising flour	**4 oz. Caerphilly cheese, grated**
Pinch of salt	**1 tablespoon snipped fresh chives**
2 oz. butter	**¼ pint milk**

Set oven to 375°F or Mark 5. Put the flour and salt into a mixing bowl and rub in the butter. Stir in half the cheese and the tablespoon of chives. Add the milk and mix to a soft dough. Turn out on to a lightly floured surface and knead, quickly, until smooth. Roll out to 1 inch in thickness, cut into about ten scones with a 2 inch pastry cutter, brush the tops with milk, put on to a greased baking tray and bake for 10 minutes until golden brown. Remove from the oven and, immediately, sprinkle the tops of the scones with the remaining grated cheese and allow it to melt. Serve warm or cold with butter.

Cinnamon Cake
Teisen Sinamon

Dark in colour and almost gingery in flavour, this is one of the most traditional of Welsh cakes.

8 oz. self raising flour	**4 oz. caster sugar**
1 teaspoon ground cinnamon	**3 eggs, separated**
Pinch of salt	**A little milk to moisten**
4 oz. butter	**1 tablespoon golden caster sugar**

Raspberry or strawberry jam

Set oven to 350°F or Mark 4. Grease a shallow 8 inch or similar baking tin. Sieve together in a bowl the flour, cinnamon and pinch of salt. Rub in the butter. Add the caster sugar and the beaten egg yolks to the flour mixture and mix well to a fairly stiff consistency. Add sufficient milk to moisten slightly. Turn the mixture into the tin and bake for about 25 minutes until cooked through. Turn out and cool on a wire rack. Reduce oven temperature to 325°F or Mark 3. For the topping, whip the egg whites until stiff and fold in the golden caster sugar. Spread jam over the top of the cake and then pile on the meringue mixture. Return to the oven and cook for about 20 minutes until the meringue is set and pale golden brown. This dessert is best eaten immediately.

Welsh Rarebit
Caws Pob

Perhaps the best known of all Welsh recipes, Welsh Rarebit is the quintessential savoury dish for a high tea or light repast.

4 slices of bread
1 oz. butter, softened
1 level teaspoon made English mustard
¼ level teaspoon salt

A shake of Cayenne pepper
¼ teaspoon Worcestershire sauce
6 oz. Cheddar cheese, grated
2 tablespoons milk or beer

In a bowl, cream the butter well and stir in the mustard, salt, Cayenne pepper, Worcestershire sauce, cheese and milk or beer. Toast the slices of bread on one side only, spread the mixture on the un-toasted side and brown under a hot grill. Serve hot. A Buck Rarebit is the same as above but served with a poached egg on top.

Butter Tarts
Tartenni Menyn

Popular throughout Wales, these delicious tartlets are a traditional teatime treat.

8 oz. prepared shortcrust pastry	**1 egg, beaten**
3 oz. butter	**A few drops vanilla essence**
6 oz. soft brown sugar	**2 tablespoons single cream**
4 oz. raisins or sultanas	**A little milk to glaze (optional)**

Set oven to 350°F or Mark 4. Roll out the pastry on a lightly floured surface and use to line 12 to 16 lightly greased tartlet tins. Melt the butter in a saucepan, stir in the remaining ingredients and spoon into the pastry cases, brushing the pastry edges with a little milk, if desired. Bake for 20 to 25 minutes or until golden. Remove from the tins and cool on a wire rack.

Welsh Scones
Sgonau Cymreig

Curranty scones that are especially buttery; a teatime treat.

8 oz. flour	**2 oz. caster sugar**
½ teaspoon cream of tartar	**4 oz. currants**
½ teaspoon bicarbonate of soda	**1 egg**
4 oz. butter	**Milk**

Set oven to 450⁻F or Mark 8. Sift the flour, cream of tartar and bicarbonate of soda together into a bowl, then rub in the butter until the mixture resembles breadcrumbs. Stir in the sugar and dried fruit. Make a well in the centre, drop in the egg and stir in, adding sufficient milk to produce a soft dough. Turn out on to a lightly floured surface, flatten with the hands to about ½ to ¾ inch thick then form into 2 inch rounds, handling as lightly as possible. Place on a greased baking sheet and brush with a little milk. Bake for 10 to 12 minutes or until golden. Cool on a wire rack. Serve plain or with honey.

Potato Cakes
Teisennau Tatsw

Originally baked on a bakestone or griddle and served hot spread with butter, Potato Cakes were traditionally eaten accompanied by a glass of buttermilk.

4 oz. flour	1 lb. cooked potatoes, well mashed
½ teaspoon baking powder	2 level tablespoons sugar
Pinch of salt	1 oz. melted butter
Pinch of mixed spice	Milk

Sift the flour, baking powder, salt and spice into a bowl, then add the mashed potato and sugar, combining well. Stir in the melted butter and sufficient milk to form a stiff dough. Turn out on to a lightly floured surface, knead gently then roll out to about 1 inch thick. Cut into rounds with a 3 inch plain cutter. Heat a buttered griddle or heavy based frying pan and cook for about 4 minutes on each side. Serve hot, with butter.

If preferred, the Potato Cakes can be placed on a greased baking sheet and baked in the oven, set at 425°F or Mark 7, for about 10 minutes.

Llandudno Fruit Cake
Teisen Ffrwythau Llandudno

A rich, fruity Celebration Cake.

8 oz. butter	2 oz. ground rice
4 oz. caster sugar	12 oz. self raising flour
4 eggs, separated	8 oz. raisins, finely chopped
1 teaspoon grated orange rind	4 oz. currants, finely chopped
1 teaspoon ground cinnamon	2 oz. glacé cherries, finely chopped
4 oz. ground almonds	4 oz. sultanas, finely chopped

Set oven to 350°F or Mark 4. Grease and line a 9 inch cake tin. Cream the butter and sugar together in a mixing bowl until light and fluffy then add the egg yolks, the orange rind and the cinnamon. Mix the ground almonds and ground rice into the flour and then add this, a little at a time, to the creamed mixture, alternating with handfuls of the dried fruit. Beat well after each addition. Whip the egg whites until stiff and fold carefully into the mixture. Turn the mixture into the tin and bake for half an hour. Reduce heat to 325°F or Mark 3 and bake for approximately 2 more hours; the cake is cooked when a skewer pushed into the centre comes out clean. Cool in the tin then turn out on to a wire rack. Leave until quite cold.

Caraway Soda Bread
Bara Soda Carawe

A variation of the ubiquitous Soda Bread; this one is flavoured with caraway seeds.

1 lb. flour	1 teaspoon salt
1 teaspoon bicarbonate of soda	12 fl. oz. sour milk or buttermilk
1 teaspoon sugar	Caraway seeds

Set oven to 450°F or Mark 8. Grease a 7 inch square shallow baking tin and sprinkle liberally with caraway seeds. Sieve the dry ingredients together into a bowl. Make a well in the centre and pour in most of the milk. Mix to a soft but not sticky dough, adding more milk if necessary. Turn out on to a lightly floured surface and knead gently for about half a minute. Put into the tin, spread out and sprinkle with more caraway seeds. Make several diagonal cuts across the top. Bake for 15 minutes then reduce heat to 400°F or Mark 6 and bake for about a further 30 minutes; the base of the bread should sound hollow when tapped. Cover with kitchen foil if the top seems to be browning too quickly. Cut into slices and butter.

Leek and Cheese Flan
Fflan Cennin a Chaws

A tasty flan served cold at teatime or hot as a light supper dish.

10 oz. shortcrust pastry	**3 fl. oz. milk**
2 large leeks	**3 fl. oz. soured cream**
Oil or butter to sauté the leeks	**Pinch of salt**
3 large eggs	**6 oz. hard cheese, grated**

Ground nutmeg

Set oven to 400°F or Mark 6. Line a 9 inch flan tin with the pastry. Slice the washed leeks and sauté them in a pan until they are just soft; season with black pepper and cool. Whisk together the eggs, milk, soured cream and a pinch of salt and then add the leeks and half the cheese to this mixture. Pour into the flan case and sprinkle the remainder of the cheese over the top. Grate some nutmeg over, place on a baking sheet pre-heated in the oven and bake for ½ an hour until golden brown. Serve hot or cold. Serves 6.

Gwilym's Favourites
Hoff ddanteithion Gwilym

These little buns, somewhat resembling rock cakes, are orange flavoured and contain chopped walnuts.

4 oz. butter	**5 oz. flour**
4 oz. caster sugar	**1 teaspoon orange zest**
2 oz. chopped walnuts	

Set oven to 350°F or Mark 4. Cream the butter and sugar together in a bowl until light and fluffy. Fold in the flour, the orange zest and the chopped walnuts to form a stiff dough. Place in small heaps on greased, floured baking trays and bake for 10 to 15 minutes until golden brown. Remove from the trays and cool on a wire rack. Makes about 20 buns.

Old Welsh Gingerbread
Hen Fisgedi Sinsir Cymreig

Despite its name, this recipe does not contain any ginger at all. By tradition the gingerbread sold at Welsh country fairs was always made in this way.

12 oz. flour	6 oz. demerara sugar
1 teaspoon cream of tartar	2 oz. chopped candied peel
½ teaspoon bicarbonate of soda	6 fl. oz. black treacle
4 oz. butter	¼ pint milk

Set oven to 350°F or Mark 3. Sift together into a bowl the flour, cream of tartar and bicarbonate of soda, then rub in the butter until the mixture resembles breadcrumbs. Stir in the sugar and peel. Warm the treacle in a saucepan, add the milk and combine well, then stir into the dry ingredients. Beat well together, turn into a greased and base lined 7 x 11 inch tin and bake for 1½ hours, covering the top with kitchen foil if it appears to be browning too quickly. Cool in the tin for 10 minutes, then turn out on to a wire rack. Serve cut into squares.

If desired, a teaspoon of ground ginger can be added to the flour mixture, though this is not traditional.

Wholemeal Bread
Bara Gwenith

A moist and sustaining wholemeal loaf sweetened with black treacle and brown sugar.

1½ lb. wholemeal flour	1 dessertspoon black treacle
½ oz. lard	1 teaspoon brown sugar
½ oz. dried yeast	Good pinch of salt
	Warm water

Dissolve the yeast and sugar in approx. ¼ pt. lukewarm water and leave to froth up. Add the treacle and salt to more warm water and stir to dissolve. Rub the flour and fat together in a bowl, then add the yeast and treacle mixtures, mixing to a firm consistency. Add more warm water as necessary but do not allow the mixture to become too wet. Turn out and knead on a floured surface for 5 minutes. Divide into two and place into two greased and warmed 1 lb. loaf tins. Slash the tops of loaves, cover with a clean cloth and leave to rise in a warm place for about an hour, until the dough has doubled in bulk. Set oven to 425°F or Mark 7. Put the loaves into the oven and bake for 30-40 minutes, until well browned. When cooked, the base of the loaves should sound hollow when tapped. Turn out on to a wire rack to cool, immediately brushing the tops with milk to glaze. Serve sliced and buttered.

Bakestone Cakes
Teisennau Criwsion

Actually rather more like scones than cakes, these traditional Monmouthshire cakes were originally cooked on a bakestone and now on a griddle or heavy pan.

8 oz. flour	**½ oz. baking powder**
Pinch of salt	**2 oz. butter**
Single cream	

Sift the flour, salt and baking powder together into a bowl, then rub in the butter until the mixture resembles fine breadcrumbs. Add sufficient cream to form a stiff paste. Roll out fairly thinly on a lightly floured surface and cut into small rounds. Lightly grease a hot griddle or a heavy frying pan and cook, turning once, until golden brown on both sides. Split in half and serve hot, spread with plenty of butter.

Teisen Lap
Light Fruit Cake

A light 'cut-and-come-again' cake with a buttery flavour.

½ lb. flour	2 oz. caster sugar
Pinch of salt	**4 oz. currants (or mixed dried**
1 teaspoon baking powder	**fruit, if preferred)**
½ teaspoon ground nutmeg	**2 eggs, well beaten**
4 oz. butter	**¼ pint milk**

Set oven to 350°F or Mark 4. Grease and base line a shallow 7 inch square baking tin. Sieve the flour, salt, baking powder and nutmeg into a bowl. Rub in the butter and mix in the sugar and the dried fruit. Beat the eggs well and mix into the dry ingredients. Add the milk slowly and beat well to make a soft dough. Pour the mixture into the tin and bake for 30-40 minutes until light golden brown. Cover with kitchen foil if the top appears to be browning too quickly. Allow to cool for about 5 minutes in the tin, then turn out on to a wire rack. Best eaten fresh.

Welsh Buns
Byniau Cymreig

Round curranty buns, made with a yeast dough.

12 oz. strong flour   Pinch of salt   ¼ oz. dried yeast
½ teaspoon caster sugar   1½ oz. butter   4 fl. oz. milk
1 egg, beaten   1 oz. sugar   2 oz. currants
Sugar dissolved in warm milk, to glaze

Sift the flour and salt into a bowl. Cream the yeast with the sugar. Put the butter and milk in a saucepan and heat gently until the milk is lukewarm and the butter melted. Add to the yeast mixture and stir until blended. Make a well in the flour, pour in the yeast mixture and beaten egg then, with the hand, beat well until the dough leaves the side of the bowl. Form into a ball, cover the bowl with a teacloth and leave in a warm place until doubled in bulk. Turn out on to a lightly floured surface and knead well. Mix together the sugar and currants and knead into the mixture. Divide into 10 to 12 pieces and form each into a neat round. Set oven to 450°F or Mark 8. Place on a greased baking sheet, cover with a teacloth and leave to prove for about 10 minutes. Bake for 10 to 15 minutes or until golden. Remove from the oven, brush with glaze and return for a further 2 to 3 minutes. Cool on a wire rack. Serve split and spread with butter and honey or jam.

Thirty

Aberffraw Cakes
Teisennau Aberffraw

Named after Aberffraw in Anglesey, once famous as a residence of the Welsh princes, these sweet, biscuit-like little cakes are traditionally cut out using a small scallop shell.

4 oz. butter (ideally unsalted) **6 oz. flour**
2 oz. caster sugar **A little extra caster sugar**

Set oven to 350°F or Mark 4. Cream the butter and sugar together in a bowl until fluffy, then gradually stir in the flour. Turn out on to a lightly floured surface, knead gently, then roll out until about ½ to ¾ inch thick. With a clean, lightly floured scallop shell, cut out the cakes and arrange on a lightly buttered baking sheet. Bake for 10 to 15 minutes or until pale gold in colour. Dust with caster sugar while still hot, then cool on a wire rack. Serve plain or accompanied by whipped cream and raspberry jam.

If preferred, Aberffraw Cakes can be cut out in rounds with a 3 inch plain or fluted cutter.

Welsh Cheesecakes
Teisen Gaws Gymreig

These delicious little tartlets contain a filling of raspberry jam topped with a light sponge mixture.

4 oz. prepared shortcrust pastry
Raspberry jam
1½ oz. butter
1½ oz. caster sugar
1 egg, beaten

A few drops vanilla essence (optional)
3 oz. flour or 1½ oz. flour and
  1½ oz. ground rice
½ teaspoon baking powder
A little sifted icing sugar

Set oven to 425° F or Mark 7. Roll out the pastry on a lightly floured surface and use to line 9 or 10 lightly greased and floured tartlet tins. Place a little raspberry jam in the base of each pastry case. Cream the butter and sugar together in a bowl until fluffy, then add the beaten egg, a little at a time, beating between each addition. Stir in the vanilla essence, if desired. Sift the flour and baking powder together and fold in, together with the ground rice, if used. Combine well and divide the mixture between the pastry cases. Bake for 15 minutes, until well risen and golden. Cool on a wire rack and serve dusted with sifted icing sugar.

Onion Cake
Teisen Nionod

This traditional dish can be served on its own for high tea or supper, or as an accompaniment to hot or cold meat at lunch or dinner. It goes particularly well with lamb, which would sometimes be roasted sitting on top of the Onion Cake. In South Wales it is called Winwns.

1½ to 2 lb. potatoes, weighed before peeling   4 oz. butter
4 large onions, peeled and chopped   Salt and black pepper
A little melted butter

Set oven to 375°F or Mark 5. Peel the potatoes, slice thinly and place a neat layer over the base of a well buttered 6 to 7 inch cake tin. Sprinkle over a layer of onion then dot with butter and season. Continue in this way, finishing with a layer of potato. Brush with melted butter and cover with a piece of kitchen foil. Cook for 1 hour, removing the foil 15 minutes before the end of the cooking time. Turn out carefully on to a warm serving dish, cut into slices and serve accompanied by cheese and crusty bread. Serves 4 to 6.

If preferred, Onion Cake can be cooked in a shallow ovenproof dish and served straight from this, though it is more traditional to serve it sliced as a cake.

Seed Loaf
Bara Carawe

A popular 'cut-and-come-again' cake that is particularly delicious when served lightly toasted and spread with butter.

8 oz. flour	**6 oz. caster sugar**
½ teaspoon baking powder	**3 eggs, beaten**
6 oz. butter	**2 teaspoons caraway seeds**

4 tablespoons milk

Set oven to 350°F or Mark 4. Sift the flour and baking powder together. Cream the butter and sugar together in a bowl until fluffy. Add the beaten eggs and flour alternately to the butter mixture, beating until well combined and fluffy, then stir in the caraway seeds and milk and turn into a greased and lined 1½ lb. loaf tin. Bake for 1¼ to 1½ hours, covering the top with kitchen foil if it appears to be browning too quickly. Allow to cool in the tin for 5 minutes, then turn out on to a wire rack.

Anglesey Cake
Teisen Sir Fôn

A light and economical farmhouse fruit cake.

4 oz. butter	Pinch of salt
4 oz. sugar	4 oz. currants
1 egg, beaten	4 oz. sultanas
8 oz. self raising flour	Milk

Set oven to 350°F or Mark 4. Cream the butter and sugar together in a bowl until fluffy, then beat in the egg. Sift the flour and salt together and fold in, then stir in the dried fruit and add sufficient milk to give a soft, dropping consistency. Turn into a greased and lined 6 inch cake tin and bake for 45 minutes to 1 hour, covering the top with kitchen foil if it appears to be browning too quickly. Cool in the tin for 15 minutes then turn out on to a wire rack.

Crumpets
Cramwythau

These crumpets are made with a sweetened batter and resemble drop scones. They are best eaten nice and hot.

½ lb. flour	¼ teaspoon bicarbonate of soda
1 small egg	2 oz. brown sugar
½ pint milk	

Put the dry ingredients together in a bowl. Beat the egg well and add the milk to it. Add the liquid gradually to the flour mixture and mix carefully until smooth. Heat a griddle or heavy based frying pan, grease and wipe off the excess with kitchen paper. Pour a full tablespoon of the batter on to the griddle for each crumpet. When the bubbles rise and burst, turn over with a slice and brown the reverse. Put aside the cooked crumpets on a hot plate and cover with a clean tea towel to keep hot until complete. To serve, spread with butter, sprinkle with sugar and eat hot. Makes about 12 crumpets.

Penbryn Cheese Pudding
Pwdin Caws Penbryn

This light, soufflé-like cheese pudding makes a tasty and surprisingly filling high tea dish.

4 oz. Penbryn cheese, grated
(strong Cheddar cheese is
an acceptable substitute)
3 oz. fresh breadcrumbs
Good pinch of mustard powder

1 oz. butter
2 eggs
Salt and pepper
½ pint milk

Set oven to 350°F or Mark 4. Separate the eggs and beat the yolks lightly in a mixing bowl. Warm the milk and add to the eggs, together with the butter and the good pinch of mustard powder. Mix well and stir in the breadcrumbs and most of the cheese. Season. Whip the egg whites stiffly and fold into the mixture. Pour the mixture into a buttered pie dish and sprinkle over the remaining grated cheese. Cook for 30-40 minutes until well risen, golden brown and just set in the middle. Serve with buttered crusty bread. Serves 4.

Treacle Scones
Sgonau Triog

Wholemeal flour and black treacle are a popular Welsh mixture, here used to make well-flavoured scones.

12 oz. self raising light wholemeal flour	**1 dessertspoon black treacle**
	½ teaspoon salt
3 oz. butter	**7 fl. oz. milk (approximately)**

Set oven to 400°F or Mark 6. Add the salt to the flour in a mixing bowl and rub in the butter until the mixture resembles breadcrumbs. Stir in the treacle and enough milk to make a soft dough. Roll out gently on a floured surface to about 1-1¼ inches in thickness and cut into rounds with a 2 inch pastry cutter. Place on a greased and floured baking tray and bake at the top of the oven for 10-15 minutes. Cool on a wire rack. Serve the scones cut in half and buttered; they are delicious with lemon cheese.

On the Ithon near Llandrindod Wells

Rice Griddle Cakes
Teisennau Reis ar y Radell

These griddle baked cakes contain boiled rice – a rather unusual ingredient.

4 oz. pudding rice	3 oz. sugar
4 oz. flour	½ oz. butter, softened
1 teaspoon baking powder	1 small egg, beaten
Pinch of salt	Milk

Boil the rice in unsalted water until cooked and then drain VERY thoroughly. Sift the flour, baking powder and salt together into a bowl, then rub in the butter until the mixture resembles breadcrumbs. Stir in the sugar and the rice, then add the egg and sufficient milk to make a soft dough that will drop easily off a tablespoon. Heat a buttered griddle or heavy based frying pan then drop on tablespoons of the mixture and cook for 5 to 6 minutes, turning once, until golden. Serve warm, plain or with butter.

Carmarthen Yeast Cake
Teisen Furum Caerfyrddin

This is a rich, yeasted cake, traditionally baked in a loaf tin.

8 oz. flour	**3 oz. caster sugar**
1 level teaspoon mixed spice	**1 tablespoon golden syrup**
Pinch of salt	**1 egg**
4 oz. currants	**5 fl. oz. milk**
4 oz. sultanas	**¼ oz. dried yeast**
1½ oz. butter	**½ teaspoon bicarbonate of soda**
1½ oz. lard	**A little milk, to glaze**

Sift together the flour, spice and salt, then stir in the dried fruit. In a bowl beat together the butter, lard and sugar until light and fluffy, then add the syrup and egg and combine VERY well. Warm the milk and divide in half. Stir the yeast into one half of the milk and leave until frothy, then stir the bicarbonate of soda into the other half. Add both milk mixtures to the butter mixture and beat well. Fold in the flour mixture and mix to form a soft dough. Place in a greased 1½ to 2 lb. loaf tin, cover with a clean teacloth and leave in a warm place until doubled in bulk; this can take about 30 minutes. Set oven to 400°F or Mark 6. Bake for 1½ to 1¾ hours, covering the top with kitchen foil if it appears to be browning too quickly. Glaze while still warm, cool in the tin for 5 minutes, then turn out on a wire rack.

Honey and Ginger Cake
Teisen Fêl a Sinsir

Welsh honey often has the subtle and delicious taste of wild thyme.

7 fl. oz. honey
3 oz. butter
12 oz. flour
1 teaspoon bicarbonate of soda
Pinch of salt

1 level dessertspoon ground ginger
4 oz. glacé cherries, washed, dried and
lightly floured or 2 oz. glacé cherries
and 2 oz. sultanas
3 eggs

3 tablespoons milk

Warm the honey in a saucepan, add the butter and stir gently until blended. Allow the mixture to cool a little. Set oven to 325°F or Mark 3. Sift together into a bowl the flour, bicarbonate of soda, salt and ginger. Take half the glacé cherries and, with sultanas if desired, add to the flour mixture. Beat the eggs and milk together, blend with the honey mixture and then add to the dry ingredients, a little at a time, beating well after each addition. Turn into a greased and lined 8 inch square cake tin and bake for 1¼ to 1½ hours, until firm to the touch, covering the top with kitchen foil if it appears to be browning too quickly. Cool in the tin for 5 minutes, then turn out on to a wire rack. This cake, if stored in an airtight tin, keeps well.

Welsh Soda Cake
Teisen Soda Gymreig

An economical, farmhouse fruit cake that uses bicarbonate of soda as its raising agent. Traditionally, sour milk would be used rather than fresh.

8 oz. flour	4 oz. caster sugar
Pinch of salt	6 oz. currants
Pinch of ground nutmeg (optional)	¼ pint milk
4 oz. butter	1 egg

1 teaspoon bicarbonate of soda

Set oven to 375°F or Mark 5. Sift together into a bowl the flour, salt and nutmeg, if desired, then rub in the butter until the mixture resembles breadcrumbs. Stir in the sugar and currants. Reserving 1 tablespoon of the milk, beat the remainder together with the egg and stir into the dry ingredients to form a soft mixture. Mix the bicarbonate of soda into the reserved milk and stir in, then turn the mixture into a greased and base lined 7 inch round cake tin, smoothing over the top, and bake for 20 minutes. Reduce the heat to 350°F or Mark 4 and bake for a further 30 minutes, covering the top with kitchen foil if it appears to be browning too quickly. Cool in the tin for 5 minutes, then turn out on to a wire rack.

Fishguard Gingerbread
Bisgedi Sinsir Abergwaun

Gingerbread is said to be one of the oldest known cakes in the world, and this fruited version, named after the Pembrokeshire seaport, is lighter in texture than most, due to the inclusion of sour milk.

4 oz. butter	**½ teaspoon salt**
3 oz. soft brown sugar	**1 teaspoon ground ginger**
1 egg, beaten	**½ teaspoon bicarbonate of soda**
5 fl. oz. black treacle	**¼ pint sour milk**
12 oz. self raising flour	**5 oz. raisins or sultanas**

Set oven to 350°F or Mark 4. Cream the butter and sugar together in a bowl until fluffy, then stir in the beaten egg and treacle. Sift together the flour, salt and ginger and add to the mixture, combining well. Dissolve the bicarbonate of soda in the sour milk and beat in, then stir in the raisins or sultanas. Turn into a greased and base lined 7 x 11 inch tin and bake for 40 minutes. Cool in the tin for 10 minutes, then turn out on to a wire rack. Serve cut into fingers.

METRIC CONVERSIONS

The weights, measures and oven temperatures used in the preceding recipes can be easily converted to their metric equivalents. The conversions listed below are only approximate, having been rounded up or down as may be appropriate.

Weights

Avoirdupois	Metric
1 oz.	just under 30 grams
4 oz. (¼ lb.)	app. 115 grams
8 oz. (½ lb.)	app. 230 grams
1 lb.	454 grams

Liquid Measures

Imperial	Metric
1 tablespoon (liquid only)	20 millilitres
1 fl. oz.	app. 30 millilitres
1 gill (¼ pt.)	app. 145 millilitres
½ pt.	app. 285 millilitres
1 pt.	app. 570 millilitres
1 qt.	app. 1.140 litres

Oven Temperatures

	°Fahrenheit	Gas Mark	°Celsius
Slow	300	2	150
	325	3	170
Moderate	350	4	180
	375	5	190
	400	6	200
Hot	425	7	220
	450	8	230
	475	9	240

Flour as specified in these recipes refers to Plain flour unless otherwise described.